THEN & NOW

HOLLYWOOD

HOLLYWOOD

Hollywood Historical Society

This book is dedicated to the people of Hollywood, Florida, past, present, and future.

ISBN 978-0-7385-6718-1

Library of Congress control number: 2008934426

Published by Arcadia Publishing
Charleston SC, Chicago IL, Portsmouth NH, San Francisco CA

Printed in the United States of America

For all general information contact Arcadia Publishing at:
Telephone 843-853-2070
Fax 843-853-0044
E-mail sales@arcadiapublishing.com
For customer service and orders:
Toll-Free 1-888-313-2665

Visit us on the Internet at www.arcadiapublishing.com

On the Front Cover: To entertain visitors to his new city, founder J. W. Young held many varied events, such as this Fourth of July 1923 baby parade on the brand-new Broadwalk paralleling the Atlantic Ocean. The babies and parents (none identified) are heading south from the Hollywood Land and Water Company sales pavilion that stood between Garfield and Arthur Streets. On that site today, behind the flag (center left, top), is the newly opened Charnow Park for children. (Then image, Wohl donation.)

On the Back Cover: In this Fourth of July 1925 photograph, city founder Young strove to impress visitors by means of a rousing marching band on Hollywood's hundred-foot-wide Boulevard, and two modern hotels. A movie cameraman records the event, looking east across the circle. Today Hollywood Boulevard is divided and planted with trees. The fate of the 1924 Great Southern Hotel (center, right) is uncertain, while the city's first hotel, the Spanish-Moorish 1922 Park View Hotel (center distance) has been demolished.

Contents

Acknowledgments

This book will explore the riches of the collection of historic photographs donated to the Hollywood Historical Society since its founding in 1974. Thanks to the forward thinking of Hollywood pioneers, hundreds of images from the 1920s, when the city was being built, have been saved in the historical society's archives. Since then, many others have generously donated photographs and postcards of Hollywood during its entire 85-year history. Such donations continue; the collection in the research center now numbers some 18,000 items. Images in the book appear courtesy of the Hollywood Historical Society, unless otherwise noted. Listed below are the donors, lenders, and photographers (when known) of the images included in this book:

Donors of Images: The Boca Raton Historical Society, Michael Chrest, Kay Rossman Ellington, C. B. Elliott/Virginia Elliott TenEick, J. W. Frehling, John Gerard, the *Hollywood Sun-Tattler*, Charles La Favre, J. F. Leonard, Regina Melville, Mrs. A. C. (Lamora) Mickelson, Harriett Ransom, T. C. Rossman, Cedric Start, Ella Jo Stollberg, Raymond Thompson, Official U.S. Navy Photograph, Laura Willis, and Thomas Wohl. All photographs with no source mentioned are in the collection of the Hollywood Historical Society from unknown sources and photographers.

Lenders of Images: ArtsPark at Young Circle, Denyse Cunningham at the Broward County Historical Commission, City of Hollywood Records and Archives Division, Paul Dumont, Elsie Johns, Memorial Healthcare System, Bill Schaaf, the *Seminole Tribune,* and Westin Diplomat Resort and Spa.

Photographers: Artvue Post Card Company, Vincent J. Ferraro, T. N. Gilbert, Max Gravis, Walter Gray, Guno Karlberg, Bill Koenig, Gary J. Kufner, Lumitone Photo Print, Nola, Alcide Pinard, Karin Richter, G. W. Romer, Schwarm and Sheldon, Earl J. Sellard, Jim Urick, Bill Veering, Vitelli, Yale Studio, and George L. Young.

Contemporary photographers: Patti Clempson, John Hayes, Joan Mickelson, Jean Shulman, and chauffeur Marion Fording.

We are also grateful for the kind assistance of Mary Beth Busutil, the photography staff at the Plantation CVS, Patricia M. Smith, and Charles Stone at Golf Hollywood! The creation of this book in Hollywood was carried out entirely by volunteers, and all author royalties will go to support the mission of the Hollywood Historical Society.

INTRODUCTION

Hollywood, Florida, founded in 1920, began as the vision of one man, Joseph Wesley (J. W.) Young Jr. (1882–1934). While living in Indianapolis, Young, already a land developer, met up with Carl Fisher, creator of Miami Beach, which inspired him to visit southeast Florida to look for a site for the city he imagined creating. In the palmetto-covered empty land between Dania and Hallandale, Young found it. On this initial flat square mile, he was able to envision a livable city with a symmetrical plan centered upon a wide east-west boulevard. Two man-made lakes would be created from a tidal marsh. Three splendid hotels (to rival those of Henry Flagler) would provide impressive vistas at either end of the boulevard, with the third overlooking the central Circle Park. These and other planned amenities were derived from then-popular City Beautiful ideals, a nationwide early-20th-century city-planning concept that spacious, park-like cities made for healthy, productive citizens. Young's city included the barrier island, which he also purchased and opened in 1922.

Young chose the name Hollywood because he liked it, not because of any fascination with movies (and the movie Hollywood was in its infancy in 1920). Young's Hollywood literally began where his boulevard crossed the only travel routes, the Dixie Highway and the Florida East Coast Rail Road (FEC), and his original city extended from about Fourteenth Avenue to Twenty-eighth Avenue; to the east and west was water. Creating North and South Lakes and the residential Lakes section was a remarkable feat of drain-and-fill engineering, lasting until 1925. A small river in the West Marsh at about Thirtieth Avenue was contained, later to become the C-10 Canal. Young named his streets for U.S. presidents (which helped local children learn the presidential names in order from George Washington to Calvin Coolidge). From the beginning, the central city had streets, sidewalks, electricity, water, telephones (if desired), trash collection down alleys behind buildings, street lighting, and lifeguards on the beach—all the latest city enhancements.

Young also decided to give his city a unified look in its architecture. When he was in his 20s, he lived in Southern California, where the newest forms of architecture were Mission-Revival, based on a new fascination with the old Spanish missions, and the craftsman bungalow as designed by the Greene brothers from Pasadena. Therefore he had his architectural firm, Rubush and Hunter, draw up pages of plans for homes and offices in the styles that he would accept in his city. These included the bungalow, Mission-Revival, Western adobe, and Spanish-Moorish styles. Few of the buildings constructed under Young's guidelines in the early 1920s have failed to survive 80 years of storms. With their now-historic facades, wood floors, exposed beams, and colorful Spanish or Cuban tiles, Hollywood homes such as these continue to charm both buyers and architecture tourists.

From 1921 through 1925, properties sold at an astonishing rate. Young built six hotels and numerous civic buildings while contractors built businesses, mostly along Hollywood Boulevard, and homes, chiefly in the Central and Lakes sections. The population soared to about 20,000, including some permanent residents who were building the city and some vacation-home owners. In 1925, the city of Hollywood was incorporated, and Young began developing his Hollywood Hills section, from about Thirty-first Avenue to Forty-sixth Avenue, creating the third and final circle at Fortieth Avenue. However, the massive 1926 hurricane and flood frightened away so many that the population dropped to about 2,000. Land was forfeited, homes were abandoned, and money ceased to flow. The national Depression came early to south Florida, and Young was unable to continue building his city.

Not everyone abandoned Hollywood. The stalwarts who remained took turns on the city commission and chamber of commerce, and, following Young's lead, lured visitors with a particular focus on Hollywood's beach. The grand and beautifully decorated and landscaped Hollywood Beach Hotel was the main draw (employing many Hollywood residents). Throughout the 1930s, the beach became filled with one- and two-story family-owned apartments and handsome vacation homes designed in the most contemporary international, or streamline, modern style, from about Arthur Street down to Washington Street. Though rapidly being overwhelmed by multistory towers, many of these charming dwellings remain in central Hollywood as well as on the beach. To the west, just beyond State Road 7, large dairies filled the grasslands, and beyond Route 27 was unspoiled Everglades.

World War II brought the U.S. Navy to Hollywood, with an officers' training school in the Beach Hotel and an air-gunners school in the Hills Inn, which by then belonged to the Riverside Military Academy. Many navy wives came, too, occupying dwellings around the city. Following the war, new construction began on the many lots left empty by the Depression, and these created Hollywood's stock of what are now called Mid-Century modern homes.

All this time, Hollywood west of Thirty-first Avenue remained empty, except for Riverside on the third circle and a few homes among the palmettos and jack pines. Finally, in 1960, Hollywood Hills (to Fifty-sixth Avenue) was opened for home building by Hollywood, Inc., on city blocks laid out by Young's company 35 years earlier. Gradually, Hollywood became incorporated west to about Seventieth Avenue. The dairies closed, and the rangeland became housing developments and malls. Today Young's dream city has grown in size to 28 square miles with a population of more than 130,000.

In this volume, Hollywood's beginnings under J. W. Young are the focus of the first two chapters. The next two chapters are devoted to businesses and private homes, from the 1920s through the 1950s. Hollywood farther west, being developed later, has its own chapter, even though much of it was built after 1960 and as such is not yet quite considered "historic." Finally, the chapter on recreation and entertainment harks back to Young's day since, like any good host, he firmly believed in providing recreation for his visitors and citizens with sports, music, parades, and, of course, Hollywood's beautiful beach, which is open and public from Dania Beach in the north nearly to Hallandale Beach in the south. We have tried to include important images from Hollywood's past. If there is no image of your favorite site, very likely none could be located.

Hollywood, like most of its south Florida neighbors, is a young city, just over 80 years old, and its historic buildings all date from the 20th century. Considering these "historical" may seem odd to people from areas where 300-year-old structures are preserved. However, this is Hollywood's heritage. If these sites are not recognized and preserved now, they could be lost before reaching the century mark—as too many have already been lost. The mission of the Hollywood Historical Society is preservation and education about the city's history. We trust that this book will encourage others to join us in our mission.

—Joan Mickelson, Ph.D.

CHAPTER 1

The Beginning, 1920–1926

Joseph W. Young's City and Buildings

Hollywood, Florida, a planned city, was laid out in 1920 to conform to City Beautiful ideals. This 1946 aerial photograph, taken by Bill Veering, clearly shows the wide central boulevard, with its three ornamental circles, framed on the east by man-made lakes. Hollywood Boulevard's eastern and western terminations were marked by monumental 1920s hotels, which served as vistas. (Regina Melville donation.)

Joseph Wesley (J. W.) Young Jr. began his city with a 100-foot-wide boulevard leading east from the main (and only) through road, the Dixie Highway. The November 1921 photograph of men laying white rock to create Hollywood Boulevard in the cleared land was posed to show it was 10-cars wide. Today the Boulevard downtown has central parking and tree shade. The Dixie and Florida East Coast Rail Way (FEC) are no longer main routes into Hollywood, allowing the central area to retain its historic charm.

Hollywood's first permanent building, a garage for work vehicles, was designed in Young's preferred mission style by Indianapolis architects Rubush and Hunter, and was erected in 1922 on the first street corner, Hollywood Boulevard at Twenty-first Avenue. Seventy White buses, like the one above (at left), brought sales prospects from the northeastern United States. Outgrown by 1923, the garage was sold and became the Ingram Arcade. Still standing today, it is occupied by shops and is a recognized historic landmark. (Then image, Elliott collection.)

Incorporating City Beautiful ideals, Young created a vista down the Boulevard by placing the 1922 Hollywood Hotel, later Park View, beside the 10-acre Circle Park. Rubush and Hunter's design had mission-style scalloped parapets. Amenities included meals, musical entertainment, and golf nearby. Young and his family lived here while building their house. Although this central island seems ideal for taller residential/office structures, it is now occupied by several stores. (Then image, Yale Studio, Wohl donation.)

With a population nearing 20,000, Hollywood still lacked a passenger train stop. In his inimitable fashion, Young offered to erect a station if the FEC would make a passenger stop in Hollywood. Considered the handsomest station south of Jacksonville, the mission-style depot was designed by Rubush and Hunter to resemble Young's hotels. It was completed in March 1924. Generations admired this block-long depot until it was demolished in the 1960s to widen Twenty-first Avenue. (Then image, Elliott collection.)

Young began purchasing the uninhabited beach island in 1922. To reach it he filled the mangrove marsh on the land side to extend Johnson Street, then installed a 70-foot barge for the crossing. The vintage photograph shows the newly rocked Johnson Street extension crossing the original dune to the Atlantic. Today the Intracoastal canal is much wider, there is only the underwater cable crossing at Johnson, and the land side is Holland Park. (Then image, Broward County Historical Commission.)

Once famous from Miami to Palm Beach, Young's Hollywood Beach Golf and Country Club, located at Seventeenth Avenue and Polk Street, was designed by Martin Hampton in 1923 in an asymmetrical style reminiscent of Addison Mizner, with whom Hampton had worked. Patronized by elegant crowds for several decades, it had beam ceilings and a striped-canvas, roll-back roof over the glass-brick dance floor. A victim of arson in 1957, the club's site is now used to store brush. (Then image, George Young.)

This 1925 traffic surge heading east past the Great Southern Hotel on the left, at 1800 Hollywood Boulevard, appears to be directed by J. W. Young (at right, in dark suit). Martin Hampton designed the Great Southern, Young's second hotel, with 100 rooms and a ballroom. Now shuttered, awaiting restoration, it cost more than half a million dollars in 1924. Today the downtown, tree-shaded, center island has eliminated the possibility of NASCAR-like traffic. (Then image, Wohl donation.)

Young hired Hampton in 1924 to design the Hollywood Land and Water Company's second Administration building. Located at 1949 Hollywood Boulevard, this building was grander and more spacious than its predecessor (now gone). Young's office was on the second floor, surrounded by the cartouche. During the Depression, the Piggly Wiggly grocery occupied the ground floor. Young's successor, Hollywood, Inc., had offices at the east end until the building was demolished. The newly replanted Anniversary Park, which now occupies this location, celebrates Hollywood's 50th anniversary. (Then image, Mickelson donation.)

One of three surviving hotels of the six built by Young, this building was intended as housing for Young's office help. It was also designed by Rubush and Hunter. But as soon as it was erected in 1925, the demand for tourist accommodation was so great that it became the Casa Blanca Hotel for paying visitors. Still standing at 2001 Polk Street, with the entrance moved to the south end but otherwise barely changed, it is now an assisted-living facility. (Then image, Stollberg collection.)

Upon discovering that segregation laws would prevent his black workers from living in the city they were helping build, Young bought more land along the Dixie Highway to create a black city similar to Hollywood, named Liberia. This 1924 photograph shows rock-laying for its wide boulevard, now Atlanta Street. Plans also indicate a central circle. Half the circle remains; the rest is Crystal Lake, which these apartments overlook. Liberia is now part of Hollywood. (Then image, Hollywood Records and Archives.)

As Hollywood grew, more residents meant more children. Young donated the block between Madison and Monroe Streets and Seventeenth and Eighteenth Avenues, and hired Rubush and Hunter to design an impressive Mission Revival building. Hollywood Central School opened in March 1925. The yellow-ochre stucco building had 24 classrooms, an auditorium, a cafeteria, a clinic, and playgrounds. After a 1968 fire, the building was demolished. Today's Central Elementary looks inward, presenting a near-solid wall to Monroe Street, with the entrance on U.S. 1.

Built in what was then Liberia in 1925 on land donated by Young at 3500 North Twenty-second Avenue, the Attucks School originally served black children in all grades during the segregated era. It was named for Crispus Attucks, an escaped Massachusetts slave who joined the Boston rebellion, which led to the Revolutionary War. Only this 1975 photograph of the original building could be located. Known today as Attucks Middle School, the new building serves the general community. (Then image, Bill Koenig, *Hollywood Sun-Tattler*.)

This landmark building, located at 219 North Twenty-first Avenue, was built by Young in 1924 to print his *Hollywood Reporter* and other publications. Presses were downstairs, with editorial offices above. When Young's publishing enterprises outgrew the building, Young donated it to the city to become Hollywood's first city hall and police department in 1925. Enlarged to the north and east after the city hall was moved, it became Hemingway's, then successive restaurants and clubs. Currently, it is empty.

Flush with success, in 1924, Young commissioned Rubush and Hunter to design an imposing five-story bank at 2001 Hollywood Boulevard, replacing a smaller building. It was a fitting structure for the First National Bank of Hollywood, which never closed throughout the Depression. As it changed hands in the next decades, the splendid facade was covered and destroyed. The 1989–1990 restoration intended to design the new facade in a mode sympathetic to the original concept. (Then image, Stollberg collection.)

Young's magnum opus—the 1925 Hollywood Beach Hotel—graces the east end of his grand Boulevard. Built in just 90 days, it was the largest cement structure on the East Coast. It withstood the 1926 hurricane and remained Hollywood's tourist magnet through the 1950s. It was occupied by the navy in World War II. Later defaced by a bridge ramp obstructing the west facade and a shopping arcade on the east, the building is being renovated as the Ramada Hollywood Beach Resort. (Then image, LaFavre donation.)

In 1925, Young opened the Hollywood Hills. Where the Boulevard ended at the western third circle he placed another Spanish-Moorish-style, Rubush and Hunter–designed hotel. In 1932, it became the winter quarters of the Riverside Military Academy (bottom photograph), which housed a naval-gunners school during World War II. Demolished in 1984, it was replaced by the startlingly modern, blue-lit, glass, Presidential Building, designed by Barretta and Associates for the Gampel Organization. The building is a visual magnet for west Hollywood. Surely, Young would approve. (Then image, G. W. Romer.)

Young's vision included a deepwater port. In 1924, he purchased 1,440 acres around Bay Mabel (bottom photograph). Dredging began under engineer Frank Dickey. Port Everglades opened in 1928, funded by bonds issued by Hollywood and Fort Lauderdale, which share it. The photograph above shows the port's placement in Bay Mabel (upper center). Today it is a major port of call for cruise ships, freighters, and tankers from the world's oceans, as Young anticipated. (Then image, Thompson donation; Now image, Port Everglades.)

Other Historic Civic Organizations

First Schools, Churches, and Hospitals

Hollywood's second-oldest civic association, following the chamber of commerce, is the Woman's Club. It was founded in 1922 with a focus on children's well-being. The clubhouse, located at 501 North Fourteenth Avenue, was erected in 1927 on land donated by Young. Architect Frederic Eskridge designed the Cape Cod cottage with its neoclassical entry. The clubhouse is listed on the National Register of Historic Places.

Before the Hollywood Central School was built, six children attended classes in this 1922 Madison Street "double California bungalow," as its architect-owner Homer Messick dubbed it. The teacher was Gertrude Brammer. By 1924, the house belonged to Young Company salesman E. E. Wagner, who added the stone wall. Beautifully maintained today, this historic home is still privately owned. (Then image, Frehling collection.)

To serve the anticipated children of Hollywood Hills, Young built the Hills School in 1926 on an oval at Taft Street and Thirty-sixth Avenue. It was designed by Thomas D. McLaughlin. But following the 1926 hurricane, the Hollywood Hills section failed to develop. The Riverside Military Academy used the building for classrooms for a time. In 1974, the building was demolished, over public protests, to be replaced by a new Hills Elementary School. Currently, another new school building is under construction. (Then image, Gary Kufner, *Hollywood Sun-Tattler*.)

One of Hollywood's earliest private schools, following Helen Hart's, was the Outdoor School, located at 2305 Polk Street. Pupils enjoyed small classes in the breezy open building (before air-conditioning). Pictured are Evelyn Gleason and her first graders about 1950, with Lamora Mickelson, the headmistress and founder at the window. The Outdoor School operated from 1938 into the 1970s and was accredited through high school. Today the Coronet Hills apartments occupy the one-acre lot. Two sapodilla trees were planted in the 1940s. (Then image, Walter Gray.)

With population growth recovering, following the Depression and war, Broward County chose Hollywood for the new South Broward High School in 1949 to serve the towns south of Fort Lauderdale. The earlier school was in Dania. Building on former tomato fields at 1901 North Federal Highway, architect Bayard Lukens's design included postwar trends like projecting concrete canopies, ribbon windows, and an air-conditioned auditorium. Today, greatly enlarged and updated, it is a Marine Science Magnet School. (Then image, Paul Dumont.)

The largest congregation in pioneering Hollywood, the Methodists, built the first church in 1924 at a cost of $30,000. Dedicated by William Jennings Bryan, it stood at 1804 Van Buren Street until the September 1926 hurricane destroyed the bell tower and caused other serious damage. Services continued in the partially reconstructed building until a new church was built in 1967. This second church (below) was designed by architect Cedric Start. Today the building seeks new tenants. (Now image, gift of Cedric Start.)

The small building on the far right (below) is the second First Church of Christ Scientist, built at 1532 Harrison Street in 1932 in the Doric Greek style, replacing a 1925 wood-frame building. When the larger church was built in 1950, the smaller became the Sunday school. In 1959, the Garden Club bought the small building and moved it to 3000 Hollywood Boulevard. Today it is home to the Big Pine and Sawgrass Model Railroad Association. (Then image, Bill Schaaf.)

The First Baptist Church was built in 1925 at 1701 Monroe Street, most likely from Rubush and Hunter designs along the Spanish mission lines preferred by Young. The original basilica had an ornate entrance, modified rose window, a mission parapet, and along the sides, pilasters framing tall windows. Possibly considered too baroque, the nave was simplified to straight lines when the church was enlarged to its present form, with a new entrance and bell tower. (Then image, Bill Schaaf.)

Hollywood's original First Presbyterian Church was erected in 1926 at 1600 Hollywood Boulevard. Previously, the congregation met in the Hollywood (later Ritz) Theatre. Like most of the city's earliest churches, it was designed in the mission style, with a white basilica with red tile roof and a central, arched entrance surmounted by double bell niches. The congregation grew, and in 1948, a larger building was designed by Cedric Start. Today there is an educational center in addition to the church and chapel.

Although the city and Young were short on funds following the 1926 hurricane, they built an imposing two-story city hall in 1928 on the Boulevard's middle circle, creating a fine vista from downtown (top photograph). In 1968, the 1928 building was demolished, and a larger city hall was erected. Later the public library and other buildings were added to the circle. Today shrubbery and multiple structures eliminate any City Beautiful vista at this circle. (Then image, Alcide Pinard.)

Hollywood's first hospital is now the oldest building on the beach. Located at 324 Indiana Street, it was built by Daniel Russo in 1924 from oolite limestone as a single-story home. After the second story was added, Dr. Harrison Walker operated it as the Gulfstream Hospital until 1929, when it became the Gulf Stream Hotel. Although the limestone, or coral rock, has been covered, the building's exterior remains basically unchanged. This historic building is now operated as the Coral House.

With a prescient eye to the future, the Memorial Hospital opened on an isolated site at Johnson Street and Thirty-fifth Avenue in 1953, well before the city developed west of Thirtieth Avenue. The first building was designed by Cedric Start (the Thirty-fifth Avenue entrance, below). Today this flagship of the Memorial Healthcare System covers several acres and includes special divisions such as the Cardiac and Vascular Institute, Cancer Institute, Neuroscience Center, and Joe DiMaggio Children's Hospital. (Now image, Memorial Healthcare System.)

CHAPTER 3

Businesses and Lodgings

Hollywood Boulevard after Prohibition (note the Schlitz sign far left) is still as Young planned it, with the Park View Hotel on the circle drawing the eye eastward. At left are the still-imposing bank building, Young's administration building (now a Piggly Wiggly), and, near the end, the Ritz Theatre. Noticeable at right are the two arcades and the Great Southern Hotel.

In 1922, Ward Kington placed a two-story building with street-level stores and second-floor apartments on the corner of Hollywood Boulevard and Twenty-first Avenue (above, at right). Placing his handsome building beside the only routes through Hollywood, the FEC railroad and Dixie Highway, Kington hoped to entice drivers to turn into the brand-new city. The Tea Room (note the sign far right) was an added incentive. Today, painstakingly restored, the historic structure has new tenants. (Then image, Wohl donation.)

One of Hollywood's earliest buildings, this office row, located at the southeast corner of Hollywood Boulevard and Twentieth Avenue, has hardly changed since 1923 (below) when Rubush and Hunter designed its Spanish mission architecture, as preferred by Young. The photograph with posed models was included in Young's company salesmen's books. In the 1930s and 1940s, Yaguda's Drugs was on this corner. Today, with its facade unchanged, the historic building houses a restaurant and shops. (Then image, Harriett Ransom collection.)

From 1921 to 1926, Hollywood grew rapidly. Housing was continually scarce. Homes could not be built fast enough; many new landowners camped in tents. Others saw opportunity and erected small apartment buildings like the Chelsea. The Chelsea, located at 2021 Pierce Street, was designed by architect Jack Davidon for Mary O'Sullivan. It had 12 units and was built with Young's preferred Spanish-mission roofline. Like the Chelsea, many similar 1920s apartments still remain throughout central Hollywood. (Then image, Broward County Historical Commission.)

Enterprising owner-builder J. S. Matson commissioned architect Martin Hampton to design his apartment-hotel, the Flora, directly across from Hampton's splendid Country Club. Costing $60,000, the Flora opened in May 1924. It was located at 1656 Polk Street and included Hampton's trademark square-tower element at the front, with eight family suites for four each, all with baths. The building may be seen in many 1920s aerial photographs of the growing city. Beautifully landscaped and maintained, the Flora today is condominiums.

The Fountain Court Apartments, located at 813–17 Tyler Street, were among the first built east of Eleventh Avenue after the east marsh was drained and filled to create the Lakes section. The builder was Eric Skogland, whose own home was located at 1025 Tyler Street (now gone). Considered elegant apartment living, the units had balconies and water views. Though the balconies and entrance pavilion have been removed (below), the landmark buildings are remarkably unchanged from 1926. (Then image, Earl Sellard.)

The Garden Apartments, built in the late 1920s, were advertised as "Perfect One-room Homes." They were built opposite the chamber of commerce, which stood facing Young Circle between Hollywood Boulevard and Tyler Street. Those rooming at the bougainvillea-bedecked Garden Apartments could walk downtown and to the golf course one block north. In 2006, they were razed, leaving an empty lot with a distant view of the golf course and of the Flora apartments at right. (Then image, Bill Schaaf.)

Topped by ornamental urns, the 1925 Harrison Building nevertheless had surprisingly modern-looking plate-glass windows. When erected at 1946 Harrison Street, it stood nearly alone on the block. In the distance at far left are homes on Van Buren Street. The 1924 Poinsettia/Royal Palm Hotel, located down Twentieth Avenue (far right), still stands. Helen Hart's school began here in 1930. During World War II, local citizens maintained a servicemen's club here. Today (lacking urns) it houses a bank. (Then image, Broward County Historical Commission.)

Moy's Chinese-American Restaurant (top, right center) was the only "exotic" dining in town when it opened in 1935. Its neighbors included a gas station, real estate offices, and Mackey Airlines. With its prime location, where U.S. 1 joins Young Circle at Tyler Street, the restaurant prospered and expanded under the direction of the Moy family. In 2004, Moy's Restaurant Lounge was sold, demolished, and replaced by Radius, a block of high-rise condominiums and shops (below, right). (Then image, Vitelli, *Hollywood Sun-Tattler*.)

Melina's was opened in 1934 at 2022 Hollywood Boulevard by owner Melina Tomich. Initially, it sold baby and children's wear, but by mid-century, it also sold "Corsets" and "Lingerie," as the sign indicates. Melina's niece Elsie Johns (in doorway, both photographs) succeeded her. By the 21st century, "Corsets" has been removed, although the shop still sells lingerie suitable to modern tastes. Melina's is now the oldest continually operated business on the Boulevard. (Then image, Elsie Johns.)

When the Florida Theatre opened in 1939, located at 2016–18 Hollywood Boulevard, it was the last word in modern—from the neon signs and portholes in the facade, to the subdued lighting and air-conditioning inside. All the latest movies were shown here, often as a double feature. Owner Paul Robinson also held war bond drives during World War II and occasionally local stage shows. After a fire, the theater was razed. The site of this pleasant meeting place is now a parking lot.

The Washburn family decorated their florist shop windows at 2002 Hollywood Boulevard according to the seasons in the 1940s, creating an appealing streetscape for strollers, as well as enticement to enter. Here is a winter scene, complete with (artificial) snow, for those nostalgic for former homes—and an exotic sight to local native Florida children. Today, with the windows screened by sedate curtains, the shop is the setting for strenuous activity within. (Then image, Elsie Johns.)

In the 1930s and 1940s, the Florida Power and Light Company had a small storefront at 1906 Hollywood Boulevard where customers could pay bills. In 1944, manager John McDonough filled his centrally located storefront windows with names and photographs of Hollywood residents serving in the armed forces during World War II (including his son) to honor National Defense Week. At the location today is Coral Shores Realty. (Then image, Guno Karlberg.)

The 1926 hurricane destroyed James Breeding's first drugstore on the Boulevard at the Dixie Highway. He later reopened at 1934 Hollywood Boulevard in the former Young Company's publishing house, which had a Venetian-style facade in 1925. When Breeding's was there, it was made geometrical, perhaps to appear more modern (above). In 2004, owners Aron and Zahava Halpern paid $500,000 to restore the building's 1920s splendor. Today this historic site is occupied by Spice restaurant. (Then image, Paul Dumont.)

The *Hollywood Sun-Tattler*, under publisher Wallace Stevens initially, served Hollywood from 1942 through 1991, covering all local news, sports, social events, out-of-town visitors, births, deaths, and city politics. At the paper's closing, the Hollywood Historical Society acquired a near-complete run in bound volumes of this key resource and a sizeable archive of *Hollywood Sun-Tattler* photographs, some of which are included in this book. All are available for research. The site at Tyler Street near Twenty-first Avenue is today a parking lot.

From the 1930s through the 1950s, numerous small- to mid-sized apartment-courts were built on Hollywood beach in the latest architectural styles, from streamline modern to mid-century modern. The Beach Crest Apartments, located at 330 Virginia Street, had smooth curved walls, sundecks, porthole windows, and entrances set off by curved planters. The apartments were probably designed by Hollywood's Bayard Lukens in the 1930s. Beautifully maintained, they are an important reminder today of Hollywood beach's mid-century architectural savvy. (Then image, Bill Schaaf.)

The Marine Deck Apartments, built in the 1930s at 321 Hayes Street on the beach, one block from the Atlantic Ocean, were another fine example of Hollywood's international-modern look. Above, the apartments are a series of geometric blocks, with shady entries created from deep, hollow insets. The buildings today still display the linear parapets and outside stairs, although the line of roof railings has been removed because the sundecks are no longer open. (Then image, Bill Schaaf.)

MONROE-PLEX – 328 Monroe Street, Hollywood Beach, Florida
Owner-Manager – Mr. and Mrs. Harold Crowells

The Monroe-plex, located at 328 Monroe Street, was built in 1949 one block from Hollywood beach, before the Broadwalk was extended south of the Beach Hotel and a seawall held back the tides. The duplex originally had decorative corner-casement windows, which opened to catch the trade winds. The low roof and double entrance steps gave the building an expansive look. Today double-hung windows enhance air-conditioning, while multistory neighboring buildings squeeze another family-owned apartment. (Then image, Bill Schaaf.)

In 1927, Mike Chrest, manager of the Tangerine Tea Room until it was demolished by the 1926 hurricane, opened Chrest's Grill and Hotel at 202 North Ocean Drive on the Inland Waterway (below). Following the repeal of Prohibition, it became a popular bar. During World War II, naval officers at the nearby Beach Hotel signed messages on the walls, which Chrest preserved. Chrest's site was eliminated when the new bridge ramp was erected. (Then image, Chrest collection.)

Joe Sonken's Gold Coast Restaurant operated from 1949 until 1994. It was accessible from A1A and the Intracoastal canal. Sonken's steaks and seafood attracted movie stars and entertainers. It was also neutral turf for major mobsters, who met there to arrange deals; their presence in turn attracted police and FBI agents. Sonken was never named a mob member, according to his 1990 obituary. Followed by other eateries, the site now houses Giorgio's, with waterside dining, boat tie-ups, and a popular bakery. (Then image, Paul Dumont.)

In the later 20th century, Martha's on the Intracoastal waterway, just south of the Dania bridge at about 6000 North Ocean Drive, was the place to go for celebrations and to treat visitors. Downstairs was informal, but white tablecloths and crystal set off the water view upstairs. Boats passing or waiting while the Dania beach bridge opened were part of the spectacle. Sadly, Martha's (at right, below) will shortly be demolished. (Then image, *Hollywood Sun-Tattler* collection.)

Three decades after Young's magnificent Beach Hotel opened, Hollywood could boast another major resort with Samuel Friedland's Diplomat Hotel, located at 3555 South Ocean Drive. Like many Miami Beach resorts, it was designed by Norman Giller in 1958 and attracted major entertainers and conventions. Eventually outgrown, it was imploded in 1998 to make way for the luxurious 39-story Westin Diplomat Resort and Spa, which was designed by Nichols Brosch Sandoval and opened 2002. (Then image, Mayer, *Hollywood Sun-Tattler*; Now image, Westin Diplomat Resort and Spa.)

CHAPTER 4

HOMES

"Group of Homes" is a page from one of the photograph books Joseph Young provided to his top salesmen. These were a pictorial document of each phase of the building of Hollywood from 1920 to 1926. Shown here were some of his preferred home styles, from bungalow to Mission Revival, dating from about 1925. Bottom right is the Kington mansion.

Among Young's earliest supporters were Ward and Minnie Kington from Kentucky. Kington bought 40 lots to develop, erected the Kington Building in 1923, and headed the chamber of commerce. To indicate Hollywood's prosperity to travelers, in 1923, the Kingtons also built this $10,000 concrete showplace (below) on the Dixie Highway at Van Buren Street. Serving as a funeral home in recent years, the Kington mansion was demolished in 2005—against local protests—for condominiums (above). (Then image, Yale Studio, Laura Willis donation.)

The first house built in Young's Hollywood was erected in 1922 from Rubush and Hunter Mission-Revival designs at 1855–57 Monroe Street. It was purchased and enlarged by Clyde and Amy Elliott in 1923. Through the 1940s, Clyde remained an active Hollywood booster, serving as city commissioner, vice-mayor, and first president of the Pioneer Club. Daughter Virginia Lathrop TenEick, a *Miami Herald* reporter, wrote the 1966 *History of Hollywood*. This keystone of Hollywood history is now endangered. (Then image, Willis donation.)

Two doors from the Elliott home is 1841 Monroe Street, presumably another of the 15 homes built in 1922–1923 by the Bastian Company using Rubush and Hunter designs approved by Young. This stucco home, with Mission-Revival parapet, bell niches, and Dade county pine floors, belonged to jeweler Frank Burton and his wife, Blanche, for many years. She taught at the Central School. Meticulously restored by present owner Ron Jakubisin, the home is a sterling example of historic preservation. (Then image, Frehling collection.)

The two homes located at 1945 and 1949 Monroe Street were built by contractor E. A. Van Atten in 1923 for the Adlers in Hollywood's Central section, the first area to be populated. Phil Adler and his wife, Minnie, chose a bungalow style (at right) while sister Hattie Adler preferred the adobe mission look. Together, they owned Adler's Ladies Wear on Hollywood Boulevard. Only slightly modified by enclosing the front porches, the homes remain today. (Then image, Yale Studio, Willis collection.)

In 1924, Young held a competition for salesmen, which was won by J. M. Jack Kagey, a Young salesman since 1920. Kagey's team sold more than $426,000, and as the prize-winning team leader, Kagey chose $5,000 over an automobile (he already owned two). The money helped build this $16,000 home, located at 1650 Harrison Street, in 1925. Later a funeral home, the mansion was purchased by the city in 1990 for more than $1 million, and it became the Hollywood Art and Culture Center. (Then image, Leonard donation.)

Though he did not win the 1924 competition, top-seller E. Emerson Evans, general manager of sales for the Hollywood Land and Water Company, also built a mansion "to show his belief in Hollywood," as Young desired of his salesmen. His beautiful 1924 home, located at 122 North Fifteenth Avenue, is still privately owned. (Then image, Stollberg collection.)

Records indicate that this center-entrance, Colonial frame house was built at 1534 Polk Street in the 1920s. The style was not one selected by J. W. Young, nor is it often seen in sub-tropical Florida. In the 1930s, with its fine view of the golf course across the street, it may have been a rooming house. Clarence and Vera Hammerstein lived here while building their home next door. The house remains basically unchanged. (Then image, Paul Dumont.)

Clarence and Vera Hammerstein moved to Hollywood from Indiana in 1927 and, with Floyd and Jane Wrays and Frank Stirling, founded Flamingo Groves. The Hammersteins were also experts in mango culture. In 1935, they had architect Bayard Lukens design this home in a style he called "Tropical Modern." The style is noted for details like the curved cement planter and variegated tile roof. Willed to the city, the historic home, located at 1520 Polk Street, is shown to the public by the Hollywood Historical Society.

Temple Methodist Episcopal Church was begun in 1925 at 1350 Harrison Street, and services were held in this imposing edifice, built of reinforced poured concrete, until damage from the 1926 hurricane, together with the national Depression, caused a loss of congregation. The building stood empty through the 1930s and 1940s (an attractive "ruin" to local children). It has since been remodeled by moving the entrance and changing the windows, and it is now a private home. (Then image, LaFavre donation.)

Post–World War II Hollywood experienced a resurgence of home construction on empty lots throughout the city. The Starrett Building Company advertisement for homes at Sixteenth Avenue and Plunkett Street (above) read "Built under F. H. A and V. A. Plan–No down payment for Veterans. Small down payment for others." These plans showed U.S. appreciation for its war veterans. Pictured below is a representative house on the Plunkett block of these timeless, adaptable Starrett homes. (Then image, Paul Dumont.)

In July 1925, Rubush and Hunter drew up plans for this baronial 23-room mansion for Joseph and Jessie Young and their sons. Said to have cost $30,000, with its eye-catching variety of rooflines and windows, it suggests the architecture of Addison Mizner, who Young knew. Two Young sons were married here. On February 26, 1934, Joseph Young died here. Jessie remained, selling the house after the war. Beautifully restored by the present owners, the multi-million-dollar mansion is for sale.

CHAPTER 5

Moving West

In this aerial view of Young's third and culminating circle in Hollywood Hills, Hollywood Boulevard enters from the left, and Rainbow Drive curves off right. Dominating the circle is the Hollywood Hills Inn, by then the Riverside Military Academy. Today this is at Fortieth Avenue. The 1940s photograph shows nothing to the west or south but watery Everglades. (Then image, Raymond Thompson donation.)

Between the Dixie Highway and Thirtieth Avenue in the 1920s were the Little Ranches, half-acre lots on higher ground, some cleared and farmed. When Young's company outgrew the garage downtown, work vehicles were moved to about 2700 Van Buren Street, to land dotted with jack pines and filled with birds and wildlife. Today this is city property where police and other city vehicles park. The west side of city hall is visible in the modern image (right center). (Then image, Raymond Thompson donation.)

In 1924, Young extended Hollywood Boulevard to future Fortieth Avenue and created the third and final circle. This photograph, called "Building Rainbow Drive," shows palm trees lining the Boulevard heading east (above, center). From the Boulevard, North Circle Drive curves around the center island to the foreground, crossing Rainbow Drive, which curves to the left. Today the area at this intersection, part of Hollywood Hills, is filled with well-landscaped homes from the late 20th century. (Then image, Leonard donation.)

A second railroad was run through Hollywood in 1926 by the Seaboard Air Line along the West Marsh at Twenty-ninth Avenue, with a station stop at 3001 Hollywood Boulevard. When early passengers arrived, beginning in 1927, they saw nothing but pines, palmettos, and marsh, with Hollywood off to the east. Today both Tri-Rail and Amtrak run on these rails, and the city continues west to Seventieth Avenue. The station is on the National Register of Historic Places. (Then image, Bill Koenig, *Hollywood Sun-Tattler*.)

The Hollywood Rifle and Pistol Club was founded in 1935 in a rock pit in farm country. In 1942, Hollywood's first chamber of commerce was moved there for the clubhouse. In 1947, two hurricanes left northwest Hollywood under standing water, including the clubhouse and Stirling Road (below). The club still operates at the same location, 2989 Stirling Road, surrounded by office buildings. Sides of the rock pit are visible in the center distance (above). (Then image, Rossman-Ellington donation.)

In the 1950s, west Hollywood was the area between City Hall Circle and State Road 7; beyond that were dairies. Town Drugs, located at 2730 Hollywood Boulevard, is shown in this 1956 photograph (below). It served a sparsely populated area, but the store was particularly popular with local politicians and workers at nearby city hall at lunchtime. Fifty years later, in 2008, Town Drug and Restaurant has a new facade at the same location. (Then image, Jim Urick, *Hollywood Sun-Tattler.)*

The Hollywood Mall, built in 1960 at 3251 Hollywood Boulevard, helped open west Hollywood to growth. At that time, shoppers enjoyed strolling along the enclosed interior "street" of this first climate-controlled indoor mall in Hollywood, free from traffic, rain, and blistering sun. With Hollywood's growth far to the west, the mall is no longer unique. The original south entrance to the "street" was removed, and various stores now have direct entrances from the parking lot.

A 1971 survey of roads clearly shows how undeveloped the city was on its then-western border. This view from Washington Street and Fifty-sixth Avenue shows that the terrain is dry, sandy ground supporting scattered pines. Today Fifty-sixth Avenue is a main north-south route. The gas station and block of shops serve a good-sized local population because there are large apartment complexes on two of the corners. At the fourth corner, in the bottom right, is Zinkil Park.

Sheridan Street was a busy thoroughfare even in 1974. However, there was not a great deal of building development here at Forty-sixth Avenue. Today this part of the Emerald Hills development (note the signpost, above right) has substantial commercial buildings on the four corners. (Then image, Karin Richter.)

Well west of incorporated early Hollywood, beyond today's State Road 7, dairy farmers opened extensive ranges in the late 1920s. By the 1930s, some 10 dairies stretched along west Broward County, including those of McArthur, Goolsby, and Wachtstetter. Today the dairy land has been developed. Last to go, in the 1990s, was the dairy Wiley Waldrep began in 1928. The barn (below), located off today's Taft Street, was replaced by the Iglesia Bautista Hispana (above). (Then image, *Hollywood Sun-Tattler*.)

CHAPTER 6

Recreation and Entertainment

J. W. Young believed in lively entertainment for his visitors and hired musicians, including Caesar La Monaca's Hollywood band. Posed here in their hussar-style uniforms with bandleader La Monaca standing at center, they are pictured alongside the casino pool. In 1926, the band played for days, helping to encourage hurricane survivors in the ravaged city and earning their deep gratitude. (Then image, Mickelson collection.)

In the mid-1920s, at the peak of Hollywood's boom, thousands flocked to the beach to promenade on the Broadwalk, dance at the Tangerine Tea Room (above, building at left), swim, and even go on wheels. The 1925 photograph shows dressed-up passengers relaxing in cabs resembling buggies with a driver who pedaled from behind (center). Today several small shops have replaced the tea room at the corner of Johnson Street and the Broadwalk (looking north), and the group bikes are now self-propelled.

When Young opened Hollywood beach, he immediately documented it in photographs that were included in his salesmen's books. In the 1923 photograph, the well-dressed beachgoers seem uncertain what to do at the beach, with the exception of the numerous swimmers. Beachgoers today, who come from many foreign countries year-round, bring blankets, chairs, toys, picnics, rafts, noodles, boogie boards, and sunscreen. They may also rent umbrellas, windbreakers, and parasails, or bring their own beach entertainment. (Then image, Wohl collection.)

The 1925 Olympic-sized saltwater Hollywood Beach Casino pool was a grand extravaganza, surrounded by 100 changing cabanas with wading pools on either side. Designed for Young by Martin Hampton, it was not for gambling but for swimming, diving, and spectator events. In the next three decades, most local children learned to swim there. Gradually, parts were removed until, in the 1960s, the remaining pool was eliminated. The site awaits development. (Then image, Yale Studio.)

In 1924, Young built an open theater at Johnson Street on the ocean to provide free entertainment for his visitors. A somewhat flimsy frame structure, it was enhanced by the poetic name Theater under the Stars. The photograph includes a photographer (above, center), who was surely hired by Young to document everything. In 1950s photographs, the site is empty. Subsequently, the city erected the more substantial Hollywood Beach Theatre, where free outdoor entertainment is still enjoyed. (Then image, Boca Raton Historical Society donation.)

This 1924 Inland Waterway event, showcasing two sleek racing boats, was observed by a crowded sightseeing boat and documented by Young's official photographer, Yale Studio. Perhaps famous race-boat builder Gar Wood was performing. This view looks west to uninhabited North Lake, which is being dredged. Related photographs include a grandstand on the beach side, which also lacks buildings. Today North Lake is ringed with mansions, while boaters of all kinds maintain low speeds to protect canal banks and manatees. (Then image, Yale Studio, Wohl collection.)

During the Depression, the struggling city of Hollywood sought to attract winter visitors with summer sports. Paddleball and tennis courts were built in 1933 on the site of the Young company's sales pavilion at Garfield Street. The wood-frame backboards (below, center left) were on Surf Road, with the Broadwalk and ocean beyond. Now with cement backboards and in near-continuous use, the newly expanded courts remain a popular beach attraction in 2008.

Bicycling has long been popular in Hollywood, and in the 1930s, Mike Chrest, an active city booster, seems to have set up this delightful scene of carefree bikers to attract tourists. The four unidentified ladies in their stylish 1930s haircuts are pedaling away behind Chrest's grill on bikes up on their kick-stands. Today Hollywood has numerous bike paths and marked lanes around the city, although Crest's site, located at 202 North Ocean Drive, is now grass and palm trees. (Then image, Chrest collection.)

This July 1943 photograph records match play championship winners at the Hollywood Beach Golf and Country Club (names unknown). As this was an official U.S. Navy photograph from the Naval Air Gunners' School, these are either servicewomen or wives of men stationed at the Riverside Military Academy during World War II, when the country club, then private, was opened to service families. Today the club is public, and year-round golf remains a Hollywood amenity. (Then image, Virginia TenEick collection.)

The Seminole Okalee Indian Village is not part of Hollywood because the tribe is a sovereign nation. However, the reservation, established in 1924, is now surrounded by Hollywood. In 1960, the tribe opened the Arts and Crafts Shop Center on the west side of State Road 7 near Stirling Road, advertising alligator wrestling with large plaster sculptures. Things have changed since the tribe built the Hard Rock Casino and Resort in 2004. It was designed by Klai Juba Architects. (Both images, *Seminole Tribune* Archives.)

Young originally planned a botanical garden for Circle Park (now Young Circle). It was a garden when the first band shell was erected in 1929. In 1950, a larger amphitheater was built that had been designed by Hollywood architect Kenneth Spry (below). Many civic events were held in the amphitheater. Fifty years later, the city remodeled its centerpiece, creating ArtsPark at Young Circle. Designed by IBI Group, Inc., ArtsPark was dedicated in 2007. (Then image, John Gerard collection; Now image, ArtsPark at Young Circle.)